THE G.I. SERIES

The War in Europe
From the Kasserine Pass to Berlin, 1942–1945

Right: Blazing away with his M1 Garand during the final fighting in Germany, this G.I. has abandoned his field pack and uses his cartridge belt to carry an E-tool, a fragmentation grenade, and his bayonet. He has slung a khaki cotton cloth bandoleer containing six pouches for carrying eight round clips of spare ammunition over his right shoulder, and has a blanket roll within which he no doubt has secured more gear as he also has done in expanded pockets.

Left: A pair of fragmentation grenades (as opposed to high-explosive grenades which had smooth outer casings) hang from this 101st Airborne 'Screaming Eagle' private's M1936 rifle ammunition belt suspenders. (Note censor's defacing of his shoulder sleeve insignia.) His M1A2 .30 caliber carbine with folding stock, a weapon often favored by paratroopers, is encased in a felt-padded canvas scabbard on his left side.

THE G.I. SERIES

THE ILLUSTRATED HISTORY OF THE AMERICAN
SOLDIER, HIS UNIFORM AND HIS EQUIPMENT

The War in Europe

From the Kasserine Pass to Berlin, 1942–1945

John P. Langellier

Greenhill Books
LONDON

Stackpole Books
PENNSYLVANIA

Greenhill Books

The War in Europe: From the Kasserine Pass to Berlin, 1942–1945 first published 1995 by Greenhill Books, Lionel Leventhal Limited, Park House, 1 Russell Gardens, London NW11 9NN and Stackpole Books, 5067 Ritter Road, Mechanicsburg, PA 17055, USA.

British Library Cataloguing in Publication Data
Langellier, John P.
The War in Europe: From the Kasserine Pass to Berlin, 1942–1945. – (G.I.: The Illustrated History of the American Soldier, His Uniform & His Equipment; Vol.1)
I. Title II. Series
355.80973
ISBN 1-85367-220-3

Library of Congress Cataloging-in-Publication Data
Langellier, J. Phillip.
The War in Europe: From the Kasserine Pass to Berlin, 1942–1945 / by John P. Langellier.
80p. 26cm. – (G.I.: the illustrated history of the American soldier, his uniform, and his equipment ; 1)
ISBN 1-85367-220-3 (pb)
1. United States. Army-History-World War, 1939–45-Pictorial works. 2. United States. Army-Equipment-Pictorial works. 3. United States. Army-Supply and stores-Pictorial works. 4. United States. Army-Uniforms-Pictorial works. 5. World War, 1939-1945-Campaigns-Europe-Pictorial works.
I. Title II. Series: G.I. (Series) (London, England) : 1.
D769.2.L36 1995

Designed and edited by DAG Publications Ltd
Designed by David Gibbons.
Layout by Anthony A. Evans.
Printed in Hong Kong.

ACKNOWLEDGEMENTS

All images used in this volume are from the National Archives Still Pictures Branch in Silver Hill, Maryland, and from the archive of Turner, Laughlin, Assoc., Ltd., Tucson, Arizona. The author wishes particularly to thank Cameron P. Laughlin for assistance above and beyond the call of duty. Without his extensive help this publication would not have been possible. Finally, I wish to dedicate this volume to George M. Langellier, Sr. and all veterans of World War II.

THE WAR IN EUROPE: FROM THE KASSERINE PASS TO BERLIN, 1942–1945

Shortly after 7 December 1941, the United States threw itself into a full scale effort as it entered the Second World War. Soon millions of men and women went into war production or entered the armed services. They would come from all walks of life and every imaginable background. Despite many differences, they would be formed into one of the most potent combat forces ever assembled.

While at first U.S. forces were heavily engaged in the struggle against the Japanese in the Pacific, mobilization brought a huge influx of men and officers, and from early 1942 many of these GIs would be deployed to the United Kingdom. The first Yanks arrived in Northern Ireland on 26 January, the U.S. Army establishing its European headquarters in London that same day.

As the months passed, more and more personnel from the United States began to assemble and train in the United Kingdom. By April 1942, American aviation units were participating in the first of what would be thousands of missions against the enemy across the Channel, and in August expanded their horizons with sorties aimed at the Axis powers in North Africa. During the next month planning for Operation 'Torch', the invasion of North Africa, focused on landing sites. On 13 September Dwight D. Eisenhower assumed leadership of 'Torch'. Within less than two months he would move his planners to Gibraltar even as the invasion force was at sea, having left Hampton Roads on 23 October.

The GIs were about to receive their baptism of fire as they came ashore with Allied forces on the Moroccan and Algerian coasts. The first American troops at Oran, a regimental combat team, made their way ashore on 8 November, opening with an unusual pyrotechnic display to announce their arrival – special red, white, and blue explosives fired from mortars which burst overhead to indicate to the French that they were facing their old comrades from the First World War. The French offered resistance before they ceased fighting on Armistice Day, 11 November.

This was only the first hurdle for the Allies, however, as they pressed on to Tunisia from the original landings, as well as deploying to Iraq and Iran. The U.S. First Armored Division was a mainstay of the U.S. component during the ensuing months of conflict. They faced stiff opposition from the Germans whom they attempted to dislodge from the Ousselita Valley, as part of the combined Allied effort now under Eisenhower as overall commander. Resistance by the Nazis with their formidable Panzers, held the invasion forces at bay into early 1943. In fact, the U.S. II Corps suffered a reverse and fell back from the Kasserine Pass, but re-occupied this strategic spot five days later, on 15 February. The cost was proportionately high: 6,500 Allied casualties against 2,000 for the Germans.

No longer untried recruits, the U.S. II Corps, under George S. Patton, began to break the see-saw pattern. By mid-March 1943 they were on the offensive, and continued so until April brought a stalemate in Tunisia. Several days later Patton was re-assigned to oversee the forthcoming invasion of Sicily. The arrival of his replacement at II Corps, Omar Bradley, essentially coincided with the momentum again turning in favor of the Allies. By May the final thrust into Tunis was achieved. Now Europe's 'soft underbelly' could be assailed.

On 9 July 1943, British and U.S. airborne forces led the way, dropping into Sicily a day before the British Eighth and U.S. Seventh Armies struck the island's south-east coast. With land forces and aviation support, the Allies pounded the defenders, the Germans sustaining 37,000 casualties while their Italian comrades in arms had four times that number killed, wounded, or captured. Realising that the battle was lost, the Germans evacuated more than 60,000 of their troops to bolster the defence of Italy, which they knew would be the next target. On 17 August 1943 the fall of Sicily proved the German high command to be correct.

Both sides now switched their focus to the mainland of Italy where in September the U.S. Fifth Army (consisting of U.S. VI and British X Corps) established a beachhead south of Salerno. A little more than a week later they linked up with British Eighth Army to form Fifteenth Army Group. Reinforcements followed, although there was a manpower shortage because of the small number of inductees mustered into the U.S. Army during the period immediately following the African campaign. The decision to land in southern France siphoned-off seven divisions, and likewise meant that reserves in Italy were precious. These factors, combined with bad weather, bogged down the Allied advance.

By now the Germans had been abandoned by their former Italian allies. None the less, they doggedly blocked the way to Rome as they dug in on the so-called 'Winter Line'. Allied progress was slow when orders came early in 1944 for the U.S. II Corps to head for Anzio, thirty-five miles south of the Italian capital. On 22 January, the attack began, the Germans being caught off guard by a seaborne assault. But the Luftwaffe retaliated swiftly and blasted the Allied forces. The advance ceased just two days after the fighting had begun, while reinforcements were awaited. The Germans battered the advance Allied units, including the U.S. 3rd Division, almost totally annihilating two battalions of American Rangers in the process. They succeeded in forcing ground to be yielded near Cassino as the struggle continued.

Naval and air support helped sustain the Allies, who faced a concentrated German counter-attack. In the process the U.S. 45th Division fell back to its final defence line, which was almost cut in half by the enemy. Then, on 19 February 1944, the tables finally turned as American tanks with artillery and aerial support

lashed back. By the next day, the enemy lines had been penetrated. The Allies not only had averted a major disaster, but also ultimately would take the offensive again, although they faced a determined enemy particularly around Monte Cassino.

As spring approached an intensified Allied thrust was launched beginning with a heavy air and artillery bombardment on 11 May. The objective was the seizure of Rome. With the combined might of the U.S. Fifth and British Eighth Armies, the plan was to break the Gustav Line.

It was the individual bravery of many fighting men that would assure victory, such as the heroic actions of Staff Sergeant Charles Shea whose regiment was in the vanguard of the U.S. II Corps as the spring offensive opened. Shortly after midnight Shea's company came under machine-gun fire which blocked their movement. The sergeant went out alone to silence the first nest with hand-grenades, then repeated his single-handed onslaught on a second gun crew with similar success. A third position opened up on Shea, but likewise fell to him. Shea's actions earned him the Medal of Honor and represents one outstanding example of the intense fighting which eventually kept Hitler's troops in check as the push for Rome continued. The prize was won on 4 June when advance elements of the U.S. Fifth Army entered that venerable city.

Scarcely twenty-four hours later another long-awaited day had arrived, the invasion of 'Fortress Europe'. On 5 June paratroopers boarded their aircraft as an advance element of the U.S. First Army and its major subordinate commands V and VII Corps, which were tasked with delivering seaborne and airborne troops to the landing sites and bridgeheads of 'Utah' and 'Omaha' Beaches, respectively. The D-Day experiences of some of these two corps' individual divisions serve to illustrate the major challenges faced by all units participating in Operation 'Overlord'.

The V Corps' standard-bearer, the 29th Infantry Division, assaulted Omaha Beach shortly after the U.S. H-Hour, 6.30 a.m. on 6 June, and secured a tenuous foothold under heavy fire. The 'Let's Go' Division had trained intensely for this day during its eighteen months in Scotland and England, and now put this practice to good use, managing to secure the beach bluff tops. V Corps' 2nd Infantry Division followed the 29th ashore on D-Day plus 1, 7 June. By 9 June, the 29th had occupied Isigny.

The VII Corps consisted of the 1st, 4th, and 90th Infantry Divisions, as well as the 82nd and 101st Airborne Divisions. The 'Fighting First', or 'Big Red One' (as it had come to be known from its First World War shoulder sleeve insignia), was a veteran outfit. It had fought with distinction in North Africa and Sicily, clearly upholding the division's slogan, 'No mission too difficult, no sacrifice too great, duty first'. In Normandy the actions of many 'dogface' soldiers exemplified this slogan, with some units suffering up to 30 per cent casualties during the first hour of the assault. Despite sometimes incredible odds, the 1st Division hit Omaha Beach and took Formigny and Caumont.

Simultaneously the 90th Infantry Division targeted Utah Beach. These 'Tough 'Ombres' of the old 'Texas–Oklahoma' Division had cut across the river Merderet by 10 June and seized Pont l'Abbé. Securing a defensive position along the Douve, the division quickly resumed the offensive with a thrust which extended to Forêt de Mont Castre, which they had cleared by 11 July.

The 4th Infantry Division, too, was slated for Utah Beach, and was one of the first of the Allied units to come ashore. The division rapidly pressed on to relieve the isolated 82nd Airborne who were hotly engaged at Sainte Mère-Eglise and in the surrounding countryside. The 4th cleared the Cotentin peninsula and took part in the capture of Cherbourg, which fell on 25 June.

Members of the 82nd had reason to welcome their 'leg' counterparts of the Fourth Infantry. Dropped hours prior to the seaborne landings, the paras' transports had scattered them all over the Cotentin Peninsula – far from their designated drop zones. The 82nd was a 'combat-savvy' outfit – blooded in Sicily before D-Day – and relied upon their internal resources during the chaos of the first days of fighting. Tasked with severing enemy reinforcement routes which could threaten the beachheads, the 82nd saw thirty-three days of unrelieved combat, fighting their way from Carentan to St. Sauveur-le-Vicomte.

Unlike the veteran 82nd, the other American division dropped behind Utah Beach, the 101st Airborne, was a 'green outfit'. The 'Screaming Eagles' (so-called because their shoulder sleeve insignia featured an aggressive-looking eagle's head in white, atop a black shield) were also dispersed in the initial drops and glider landings. They came up against staunch opposition in their assaults on Pouppeville, Vierville, and St. Côme-du-Mont. After more than a month of continuous combat, the 101st returned to England, never again to be called 'green'.

Within the first twenty-four hours, some 176,000 troops had come ashore from 4,000 ships and through airborne operations, 'being protected by 9,500 aircraft and 600 warships'. During the following weeks and months numerous Allied forces expanded the beachhead, truly widening the vaunted Second Front into a breach which the Germans could not close.

Yet, final victory was not easy or immediate. The Allies attempted to secure and consolidate their position. Towards the end of June the port city of Cherbourg fell to the U.S. 4th Division, after bombardment by air and sea, followed by street-fighting. The Cherbourg peninsula followed on 1 July, when the U.S. 9th Division reached Cap de la Hague. Soon afterwards the U.S. troops were engaged in the hedgerows in a major offensive through the Cotentin Peninsula, which one German commander pronounced a 'bloodbath', until their thrust reached the vicinity of St-Lô, where in mid-July the Americans were temporarily halted. The U.S. XIX Corps captured the town on 18 July which finally brought a conclusion to the costly hedgerow battle.

Within a week, the U.S. First Army staged a breakout from the St-Lô area. As bad weather cleared, they received extensive air support which had been denied hitherto because of heavy rains. German defences were weakening. Hitler ordered a counter offensive in Brittany. There, on 6 August, Patton's Third Army cut off and isolated four German divisions. Next day, spearheaded by massed armor, the German counter-attack towards Avranches attempted to stonewall the Allies' slow but relatively steady advance into Normandy. With these gains Eisenhower moved his headquarters from England to northern France, and on 15 August Free French and U.S. troops landed in the Cannes–Toulon area of southern France as a further threat.

In less than forty-eight hours the southern strike force had secured a 50-mile bridgehead, and pushed on to other objectives even while the

U.S. 79th Division was encircling the remaining German units holding out in Normandy. The double-edged threat pressed the Germans, who had lost 200,000 killed or wounded and the same number captured since D-Day, representing the destruction of some twenty-eight divisions in the west.

Badly mauled, they threatened to destroy Paris before the Allies arrived. Dissuaded from this drastic measure through international diplomacy, they abandoned their once secure spoils of earlier fighting. The French 2nd Armoured Division triumphantly rolled in to liberate the city on 25 August. They were followed by the Americans who came in from the south later that morning.

This forward drive slowed at the beginning of September when fuel shortages required Eisenhower to order his First and Third Armies to remain in place, while supplies were stockpiled. This circumstance allowed the Germans time to regroup along the Siegfried Line. None the less, the U.S. 7th Armored Division remained in motion, heading toward the river Moselle. A crossing had been achieved by 7 September, but the end still was not in sight.

In fact, only ten days later 'Market Garden', an operation which involved one British and two American airborne divisions in an attempt to capture the Low Countries quickly became bogged down. The clash proved costly with fighting continuing until mid-November. General Bradley viewed this clash as, 'an irrevocable logistical loss to the Allies'.

The following month brought other crucial setbacks. Hitler would not concede defeat. Despite warnings from his staff, he ordered a major counter-attack which began at 5 a.m. on 16 December 1944. This last hurrah witnessed the Germans repeating their famous lightning tactics that had won the day so often in the past. Their *Blitzkrieg* through the Ardennes Forest of Belgium severed the Allied lines at the weakest point on the Western Front. In the process, the oncoming infantry and panzers engulfed the Americans at Bastogne. The besieged defenders under Brigadier General Anthony McAuliffe would not submit, although others did, including some 8,000 men who surrendered to the Germans, 'at one time and place' which was more 'than in any other episode of the entire war except Bataan'. Before it was over more than a million men had been engaged in this struggle which came to be known as the Battle of the Bulge. Veterans and unblooded recruits on both sides confronted one another and the freezing-cold of winter in a month-long dance with death. Finally, in mid-January the Allies regained their position, causing their adversaries to fall back after the Germans had sustained some 120,000 casualties besides extensive destruction of their armor and artillery, all squandered as time soon would show.

It was now January 1945. The once mighty Wermacht and the high-flying Luftwaffe both had become shadows of their former selves. By the next month the Rhine was in sight, a barrier to be forded by the Allies. The fortuitous capture of a railroad bridge at Remagen facilitated a crossing for elements of the U.S. First Army. Others followed. Target after target fell. The 'thousand year' Third Reich stood ready to topple.

To the south, in Italy, capitulation came on 19 April 1945. The Soviets closed on east Berlin and would be met by the other Allies from the west. On 8 May Germany surrendered. Victory had been achieved in Europe. None too soon survivors looked forward to home and loved ones. GIs longed to return to peace – no more C or K rations, and no more olive drab scratchy wool or green herringbone twill.

FOR FURTHER READING

The Army Almanac: A Book of Facts Concerning the Army of the United States. Washington, DC: U.S. Government Printing Office, 1950

Ethell, Jeffrey L. and Isby, David C. *G.I. Victory: The U.S. Army in World War II Color.* London: Greenhill Books, 1995

Goralski, Robert. *World War II Almanac 1931–1945: A Political and Military Record.* New York: Bonanza Books, 1984

Howard, Gary. *America's Finest: U.S. Airborne Uniforms, Equipment and Insignia of World War Two (ETO).* London: Greenhill Books, 1994

Sylvia, Stephen W. and O'Donnell, Michael J. *Uniforms, Weapons and Equipment of the World War II G.I.* Orange, VA: Moss Publications, 1982

Above: Training stateside before deploying overseas, this paratrooper has converted his standard herringbone twill uniform by painting a camouflage pattern on the jacket and trousers similar to the pattern on his parachute. In practice, woodland camouflage patterns were seldom used, though pathfinders occasionally modified their clothing to blend in with the European terrain.

Above: In a dress rehearsal for D-Day, a platoon moves through an English village in the combat uniform that would serve for the early part of the European operations including the 1941-pattern field jacket, and the olive drab wool shirt and trousers worn with the M1 helmet.

Left: Normandy-bound troops in LCIs and LCVPs anticipate the landing in France. Painted white arcs are evident on the front of the M1 steel helmets worn by men of the Amphibious Landing Forces. In the background can be seen barrage balloons which provided anti-aircraft protection to embarkation points and the invasion fleet.

Above: Atop a 'half-track' three G.I.s in England make a last- minute check of a caliber .50 Browning air-cooled M2 machine-gun. This weapon was capable of a rate of fire from 450 to 575 rounds per minute, and could use ball, armour-piercing, tracer, and incendiary ammunition.

Left: G.I.s take time to chat with children of a Dutch village as they push on against the Germans in the autumn of 1944. Although these men are members of the armoured forces they nevertheless wear the standard 1941-pattern field jacket rather than the pattern of jacket issued to tankers. They are the four-man crew of an M5 or M5A1 light tank which has been modified with 'bocage cutters', an addition necessitated by the hedgerow fighting in Normandy. The tank's main gun was a 37mm M6 supported by caliber .30 machine-guns.

Right: In their 1941-pattern airborne field uniform and M1C steel helmet, these paratroopers prepare messages to send via carrier pigeon (held in the small round wire cage in the foreground), a means of communication which was used up to the invasion of Holland in 1944, and was part of many paratroops' equipment. The man at the right has the M1A1 Thompson submachine-gun; his comrade on the left packs the M1A1 caliber .30 carbine with folding stock which was manufactured specifically for airborne troops. The paratrooper in the background collapses his chute after landing.

Right: While the M1 'Garand' became the main weapon of the American foot soldier soon after the outbreak of the First World War, the M1903 A4 caliber .30 Springfield rifle with telescopic sight was issued to snipers, such as parachute infantry Sergeant Douglas Dillard, an expert marksman whose reversible (white side and olive drab side) poplin two-layer ski parka with fur trimmed hood provides camouflage in the snow of the French Alps.

Left: Four privates of Company F, 325th Glider Infantry Regiment, which formed part of 82nd Airborne Division, fight their way through a German street in 1945. They have all been issued with the 1943-pattern uniform, including the two-buckle boots which eliminated the need for leggings.

Right: Olive drab wool or khaki cotton uniforms were the mainstay of operations against Germany and Italy, but specialized gear was required too, as in the case of this diver with the 1058th Port Construction Company, who was engaged in repairing a railroad bridge near Aachen, Germany in March 1945.

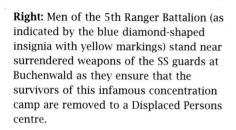

Right: Men of the 5th Ranger Battalion (as indicated by the blue diamond-shaped insignia with yellow markings) stand near surrendered weapons of the SS guards at Buchenwald as they ensure that the survivors of this infamous concentration camp are removed to a Displaced Persons centre.

Right: Major General Matthew Ridgway with his XVIII Airborne Corps shoulder sleeve insignia, wears the 1943-pattern ETO jacket which eventually became 'Class A' or 'walking out' dress, although originally designed as part of the combat uniform.

Left: Just two months after Victory in Europe, G.I.s at Le Havre, France, board a freighter for their return to the United States. They are hauling their olive drab duffle bags, an improved carrying method over the old barracks bag which they were to replace, with extra clothing, gear, and perhaps souvenirs of their service in the ETO. The duffle bag could take more than fifty pounds and had a stout web strap and a padlock for additional security.

Above: When the U.S. Army entered the Second World War training was one of the first orders of business before deployment against the enemy, especially for the newly formed airborne units, such as these men who are attired in the one-piece herringbone twill (HBT) coveralls and two types of early parachutists' helmets which resembled the headgear of American football players and aviators at the time.

Right: Taken in April 1941, this photograph of Private Arthur Payne during airborne training with the 501st Parachute Battalion at Fort Benning, Georgia, depicts the transitional paratrooper's uniform of 'balloon cloth' which was abandoned soon after the first jumpsuits of this type were issued.

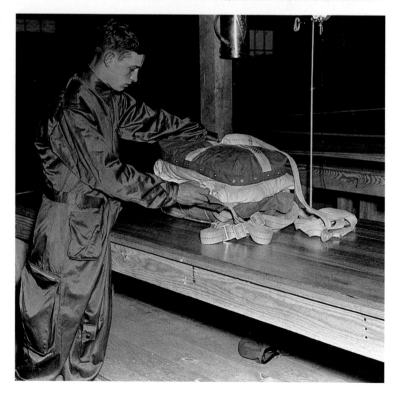

Above: Before shipping overseas considerable stateside preparation also was required as depicted by Sergeant Rosario Cannoni who is shown engulfed by small arms including Springfield .30-06 bolt actions, 12-gauge pump shotguns, and a .30 calibre water-cooled Browning machine-gun, which used eight pints of water as coolant for the barrel, and fired from 450 to 600 rounds per minute. The sergeant wears the 1941-pattern herringbone twill two-piece work suit and a matching 1940-1941 cotton field hat (sometimes called a 'Daisy Mae' in G.I. slang) with an enlisted cap insignia of sheet brass.

Left: The one-piece HBT work suit worn by these two tankers training at Fort Benning, Georgia, in April 1942 was not available in large quantities until early in the war. In order to display rank on this uniform some individuals, such as the sergeant on the right, stencilled or painted on their chevrons. The sergeant also wears a brown leather M2 hip holster but his six-shot .45 caliber revolver is not evident. The tanker's helmet with issue goggles was standard for armored forces in North Africa and Europe, throughout the war.

Above: During April 1942, still at Fort Benning in their training phase, these tankers line up for chow in their one-piece HBTs. The men serving the food wear the old style helmet inspired from British patterns and first issued in 1917 to Yanks. This protective cover, known as the M1917A1 and much modified from its World War I predecessor, would soon be replaced by the M1. The mess plate and pan M1910/17, as well as the large canteen cup also traced their design back to earlier in the century.

Above: Early in the war the one-piece HBT coveralls were phased out as an issue item for most G.I.s, except for men engaged in work as mechanics or other similar tasks, often in rear areas. In Iceland, during 1942, Sergeant Randolph Richmond feeds underground cable protecting his hands with issue work gloves and cutting the chilled air with his 1941-pattern field jacket. Note the tabs at the ankles which assisted in blousing the coveralls when worn with the M1936 canvas dismounted leggings. In this case the sergeant wears the rough out field service shoe with no toe cap, the most common type of footgear for most of the early war.

Right: Another example of the one-piece HBT, which continued in limited use throughout the Second World War, dates from 1945; Technician 4th Class (the rank being indicated by painted chevrons on the sleeves) John Warfel retreads a worn-out tire in an ordnance repair shop located in eastern France. Note that he also has added a non-regulation white label with his serial number above his left pocket for purposes of identification.

Below: Ready to embark for overseas duty in September 1942, Engineer troops all wear M1933 olive drab (OD) wool shirts and field trousers, the gas mask developed between WWI and WWII, and carry denim barracks bags in addition to their M1936 field bags.

Left: Some of the first troops to arrive in the United Kingdom included men of the 503rd Parachute Infantry, shown here in Berkshire, England, during October 1942 with painted camouflage M1C helmets and the 1942-pattern jump jacket and trousers, the latter being bloused into the 'boots, jumper, parachute' with 10-inch-high tops fastened by twelve pairs of eyelets. The T5 reserve and main chutes also are in evidence.

Right: In Europe, wearing a tailor-made 'Class A' uniform and garrison cap, a U.S. Army lieutenant general signs an autograph for a 'medic' who carries his dressing pouches as well as extra medical supplies in a kitbag suspended from a snaphook attached to a pack suspender. The aidman is kept warm by a pre-1941 style mackinaw.

Left: Despite his nickname of 'Blood and Guts', George S. Patton, Jr. was a dapper dresser. Here, as a lieutenant general, Patton strides out of his tent with glossy painted helmet bearing three silver stars and a tailor-made ETO jacket with all his ribbons. He has bloused his trousers in 'jump' boots rather than wearing standard issue footgear, and carries a swagger stick. It appears that he has slung olive drab binoculars in the M17 case over his right shoulder. Note the hook on the left front of his jacket which was used to support his general officer's custom double pistol belt rig.

Above: Looking rather crisp as he delivers a message on his Harley-Davidson motorcycle to a British Tommy, this G.I. courier has slung an M1938 dispatch case and strap over his right shoulder. He wears the 8.2-ounce cotton khaki tie which although adopted in 1939 would be replaced in 1942 by an olive drab version made of cotton and mohair.

Right: During May 1944 G.I.s practice seaborne assaults in England during the 'Fabius' exercise. They load into a 50-ft-long Landing Craft Medium (LCM) from vertical chain descent ladders over the side of their transport vessel. The officer observing the operation is distinguished by the vertical white stripe on the rear of his helmet.

Below: The G.I.s saw their first ground action against the Germans and the Italians beginning in 1942 in North Africa. Coming ashore from Coast Guard-manned 'sea-horse' landing craft, these Yanks wear the 1941-pattern field jacket and wool field trousers, although both could prove too warm given the climate in this theatre of operations.

Left: In England, during 1943, an engineer major shows a sergeant how to set up a booby trap. Both men wear the officer's and enlisted version of the garrison or 'overseas' cap respectively, in this case of OD wool. In the former instance a black mohair with gold thread intermixed piping ran around the cap and for the engineer enlisted man a red and white intermixed worsted cord was applied. Other colours designated the various branches, such as light blue for infantry, scarlet for artillery, and the like.

Below: In January 1943 a Technician 4th Grade removes .50 calibre machine-gun rounds and other ammunition from a damaged M3 (General Grant) tank. He mixes a khaki cotton garrison or overseas cap with the 1941-pattern field jacket and OD wool trousers. Behind him a man stands guard with a .30 calibre Springfield bolt-action rifle which had been all but replaced in the Regular Army by the M1 Garand as of 1941.

Above: By June 1943 these troops in Tripoli still do not have the M1 helmet, but rather continue to wear the 'Kelly Pattern' M1917A1 helmet. They all have cotton khaki uniforms as they relax in sight of their 37mm anti-aircraft gun, a weapon which had a maximum vertical range of 6,200 yards and a maximum horizontal range of 8,875 yards for its high-explosive (HE) ammunition.

Left: Inside a power generating plant to operate radar, a private first class (indicated by a single chevron) from the 90th Coast Artillery in Casablanca, during June 1943, wears a cotton khaki uniform with standard M1936 dismounted leggings, a practical work outfit for the most part in this hot climate.

Left: This same cotton khaki uniform served as the 'Class A' uniform in North Africa as indicated here during a baptism service conducted by the chaplain of the 6th General Hospital, during September 1943. Note that the chaplain on the left has loops on the shoulders of his shirt which was the pattern worn by officers while those for enlisted men were without loops.

Below: Boarding large camouflaged landing craft at Naples, this invasion force is on its way up the west coast of Italy for another landing. The M1910/1928

haversack, used as a field pack, particularly is evident with heavy blanket rolls over the top and sides.

Right: A three-man patrol from the 3rd Infantry Division enters Mignano, Italy, in November 1943. The man on the left carries a Browning Automatic Rifle M1918A2.

Below right: An M1 240mm howitzer from Battery B, 67th Field Artillery near Mignano, Italy, during January 1944. It could fire one M114 360-pound high-explosive round per minute at a maximum range of 25,255 yards.

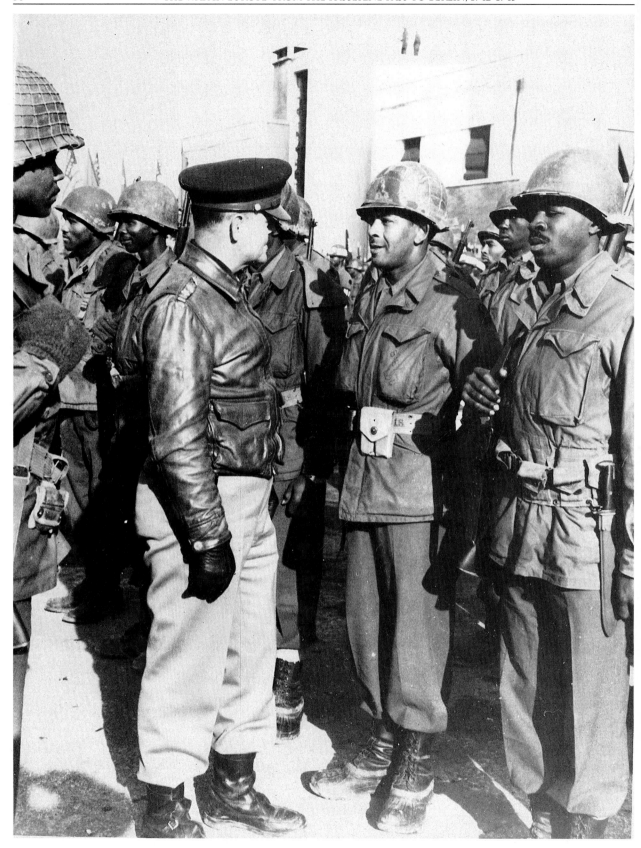

Above: Lieutenant General Lucian Truscott, commanding the U.S. Fifth Army in Italy, has procured an A2 leather or goatskin flight jacket supposedly restricted for use by aviators. His non-regulation custom buckle-on boots contrast with the 12-inch shoe pac, M1944 worn by the 92nd Infantry Division personnel he is reviewing.

Right: Wounded men from the U.S. fifth Army in the Cisterna, Italy, area assist each other off the battlefield. They wear tags which indicate their medical status. The M1910/17 canteen is suspended without its 1910/17 cover from the belt of the soldier on the left for easier access. This same G.I. has on his dog tags and OD cotton undershirt. The packed MB or GPW 'jeep' has a Thompson submachine-gun leather scabbard for use on vehicles.

Right: A combat patrol of the 92nd Infantry Division advances north of Lucca, Italy, in September 1944. In the background a man prepares to fire a 2.36-inch rocket launcher. The 'bazooka' came in M9, M9A1, and M18 types and could fire up to ten rounds per minute.

Left: Troops from the US Seventh Army hit the beaches in Italy, during 1944, wearing U.S. flags to identify the men as G.I.s. Litters indicate that this is a medical unit as does the lack of small arms which non-combatants were forbidden to carry.

Lower left: An 8th Air Force corporal and staff sergeant enjoy a visit to the Tower Bridge in November 1944. Their olive drab wool serge service coats are of the pattern issued before the war and which remained in use throughout the conflict, although they would be less prominent than the European Theatre of Operations (ETO) 1943-pattern jacket as the war progressed.

Below right: Much of the standard G.I. combat uniform for the early ETO is seen in this picture of Corporal Richard Higley who is astonished at seeing so much butter, which virtually was worth its weight in gold during the conflict. The M1 steel helmet, the 1941-pattern field jacket (which had been adopted in limited quantities in the 1930s), M1936 pistol belt, and the olive drab wool trousers with M1936 dismounted leggings and rough-out service shoes all were typical issue.

Below: Preparing for the invasion of the Continent, the 326th Airborne Medical Company, 101st Airborne Division assembles in England, during March 1944, to display the extensive supplies they must carry when going into combat to treat casualties. All have the 1942-pattern paratroopers, uniform and M1C helmet, including their captain who is second from the right and identified by a pair of vertical bars on the front of his steel pot.

Above: General Eisenhower, wearing the ETO jacket which would come to bear his nickname ('Ike'), talks to men of the 101st Airborne prior to their leaving for the D-Day. The paratroopers have darkened their faces for a night drop and wear the 1941-pattern jump uniform. The man on the right wears a grenade bag around his neck and has a white painted heart on the side of his helmet, one of the markings employed to identify men from specific units within the division.

Opposite page, top: Corporal Nick Penardo's bowler is strictly non-regulation, but is a souvenir, as is the German helmet to his right, from Normandy. His own M1 helmet is in the background on the left as the corporal heats up his rations on an individual lightweight stove. He has on the two-piece olive drab shade #7 herringbone twill trousers and shirt or jacket adopted in 1943 and which became popular for summer wear as the war progressed. The ubiquitous identification tags hang around his neck.

Right: Moving inland, on 9 June 1944, American infantry leave the comparative safety of a concrete sea wall at the Normandy beaches. In the background the men haul long tubes which are 'Bangalore' torpedoes used to breech enemy defenses.

Above: Taking cover under fire, the soldier on the right has been issued the old 'T' handle M1910 entrenching tool which is attached to his cartridge belt.

Opposite page, top: The 60mm M19 mortar packed a powerful punch with a maximum range of 784 yards without its mount (as seen here), and when used with its mount could hurl its shell up to 1,985 yards. The radioman on the right with his hand-held receiver and transmitter ('walki-talki') has the new M1943 entrenching tool suspended from his cartridge belt in this 1944 picture taken in France.

Opposite page, bottom: Fighting in St-Lô, France, in July 1944, two men operate an 81mm M1 mortar as they lob shells up to 3,300 yards. Capable of being carried by a pair of men or hauled on the M6A1 cart, this weapon was a product of WWI but carried over into WWII. The soldier on the right has M1938 wire-cutters in their carrying case on his left hip.

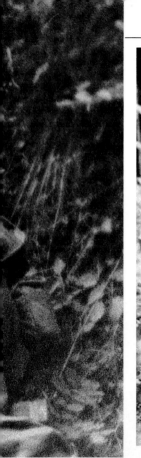

Above: Two captains (left and center) and a lieutenant of the 761st Medium Tank Battalion appear in the 'limited standard' arctic four-buckle boot and the M1943 field combat boot respectively. The captains wear the armoured forces uniform commonly seen at this time in France (November 1944), including the zipper closed jacket with knitted wool collar, wristlets, and waistband. The lieutenant on the right has pulled on green wool glove liners and donned a 1942-pattern officer's trench coat.

Right: From left to right Generals Gavin, Eisenhower, Ridgway, and Brereton appear in the service dress uniform as it came to be known late in the war, including the ETO or 'Ike' jacket. Variations in shades and patterns are evident at this review of the 82nd Airborne Division. Gavin wears the steel helmet while Eisenhower and Brereton have on garrison caps. Ridgway and the brigadier general in the rear row have chosen to wear overseas caps.

Below: Not long after breaking out from the beaches of Normandy, Corporal Earl Littlefield uses his field phone, which has been removed from its leather carrying case, to relay information from an observation post.

Opposite page: The M3 U.S. submachine-gun, often called a 'greasegun' because of its resemblance to that tool, provided a less expensive substitute for the Thompson. Paratroopers and armoured forces particularly favoured the light-weight compact .45 calibre weapon which weighed 8.9 pounds fully loaded with sling and measured 39.8 inches with its sliding stock fully extended. It could fire 400 rounds per minute although the magazine held only thirty rounds of ball ammunition.

Left: In August 1944 a G.I. from the 29th Infantry Division finds a use for a C-ration box as a shooting platform as he fights through the hedgerows of France. This source of food was designed specifically for men in combat and derived from experiments beginning in 1938. The idea was to provide three meals a day to the fighting man packed in six small cans. The ration supposedly was palatable whether served hot or cold, although the latter form was the most common. The infantryman also has obtained an M1 bayonet modified as a trench knife with an ETO-produced leather scabbard.

Above: The M9A1 3-inch gun being fired here in Belgium during the Ardennes battle was one of the many artillery types which saw service in World War II. Most of the artillerymen on the gun crew have adopted the armoured force winter combat hood of cotton lined with wool kersey.

Below: Men of the 3200th Quartermaster Service Company exhibit the array of uniforms and equipment being issued late in WWII. Both 1941- and 1943-pattern jackets are evident as are two versions of the olive drab mackinaw, field sweaters, an officer's 1942-pattern overcoat, woollen issue scarves, the woollen knit toque, the enlisted wool overcoat, and the OD wool protective hood.

Left: Corporal Charles Johnson of the 783rd Military Police Battalion waves through the 'Red Ball Express' as they roll through France, in September 1944, to rush supplies to the advancing forward lines. Military police wore brassards and often the 'MP' on their helmet in order to distinguish them as they carried out such duties as traffic control. A white T-shirt is visible below his 1943-pattern OD field jacket and shirt.

Right: An aidman from the 4th Armoured Division at Bremercourt, France, in September 1944, wears the red, yellow, and blue shoulder sleeve insignia of his outfit on his tanker's winter combat jacket which was made of water-repellent cotton with a kersey lining and knitted wool cuffs, collar, and waistband.

Lower right: Yet another medic, in this case from the 23rd Infantry Division during March 1945, attends to a wounded soldier from his unit. He has secured a pair of tanker's winter combat overalls made of canvas lined with kersey, which he wears over a 1941-pattern field jacket to provide warmth by layering his clothing, which also includes a highneck worsted wool sweater underneath, one of the 1943 additions to the combat kit. The soldier being treated is wearing the light-weight olive drab poncho with its raised collar that had snap fasteners which could be closed to create sleeves. This all-purpose item could be used as a ground cloth, a rain garment, or a shelter-half. His M1943 boot tops likewise are visible above the cut-down four-buckle overshoes.

Left: Crossing the River Arno, in September 1944, men of the 370th Infantry Regiment are loaded for bear. The man at the rear of the column carries a box with spare ammunition for the .30 calibre Browning air-cooled machine-gun, while the weapon itself is being lugged by another G.I. just slightly ahead in the same column.

Below left: As areas of France were liberated some troops could put aside their combat gear for other duties, such as this quartet who broadcast from Rennes, France, for the pleasure of their fellow soldiers, in October 1944. The Technician 4th Grade on the right has had a tailor apply his Army Service Forces shoulder sleeve insignia and chevrons on the 1941-pattern field jacket with cross hatch stitching, a detail which some men opted for to dress up their uniforms or give a distinctive look.

Below: In stark contrast to the quartet, this grizzled trio of ground soldiers halt at Luneville, France, during October 1944, for a smoke break. Their M1 helmets all have camouflage netting. The man on the right has on the M1936 rifle ammunition belt suspenders while his comrade in the centre has opted to wear his M1924 cartridge belt without suspenders. The same G.I. and the one on the right have their M1943 entrenching tools on their belts and Sergeant Kelly Lasalle (with his rifle over his shoulder) also carries a M1938 dispatch case along with a pair of captured German 6 x 30 binoculars, and the bayonet in its M8 scabbard for an M3 trench-knife, despite the fact that he is using a Garand. Lasalle also has a lenseatic compass pouch.

Left: Bundled up and singing Christmas carols, during December 1944, these 3rd Army artillerymen have on their double-breasted 32-ounce wool overcoats which closed with three brass buttons in each row (later replaced by plastic versions). This garment differed little from its WWI predecessor, except for the addition of pleats at the back, and a roll collar with notch lapels. Extra warmth is provided by the highneck 1943-pattern worsted wool sweater on the artilleryman on the right, who also has the 1941-pattern wool-knit toque (hood). His comrade on the left wears an OD wool scarf and the olive drab knit 'jeep cap' with short visor which had side flaps that could be unfolded to cover the ears.

Left: Aidmen from the 94th Infantry Division respond to claims made by the Germans that they cannot tell the difference between medical personnel and regular troops. Thus, they have added a large field adapted Red Cross vest along with brassards on both arms and markings on four sides of their M1 helmets. The non-commissioned officer on the left also wears the windproof and water-repellent poplin cloth hood with draw string closure which was adopted in 1942 to coincide with the M1 helmet's appearance.

Above: G.I.s were not the only ones to wear US-made uniforms as indicated here by men of the French First Army who raise the Tricolor of the newly liberated city of Belfort, on 20 November 1944, a strategic gateway to the invasion of southern Germany. Most of the men have on four-buckle arctic overshoes and can be distinguished from their American counterparts by the French markings on the left side of their helmets.

Below: Operating 40mm Bofors anti-aircraft guns, these troops form part of a 6-man crew required to handle this versatile weapon of Swedish design which fired 2-pound shells at a rate of 120 rounds per minute with an effective range of 12,000 feet. Originally designed for use by the U.S. Navy, the 2.4 ton-guns were fitted out with wheels and used on land to protect bridges, rear areas, and for other defensive purposes.

Right: The 57mm gun was effective against certain armour vehicles and for other limited artillery support. It had the advantage of being relatively mobile so that its position could be changed in short order as the tactical situation dictated.

Below right: The M8 Armoured Car had a 37mm gun, and two machine-guns, one in .50 calibre and the other in .30 caliber. Its 4-man crew could ride at a maximum speed of 56 mph, while the cruising range was 350 miles for this six-cylinder scout and reconnaissance vehicle.

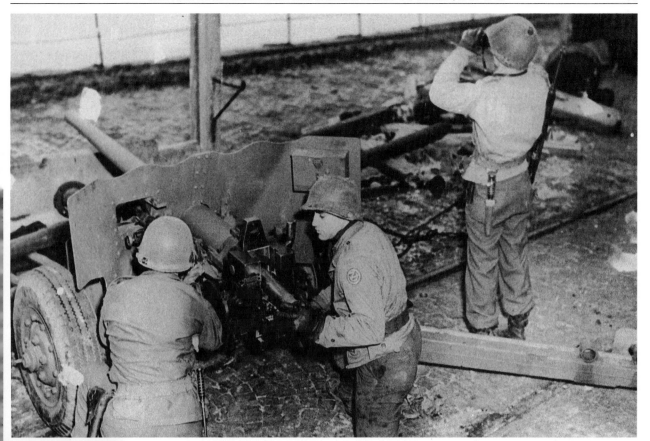

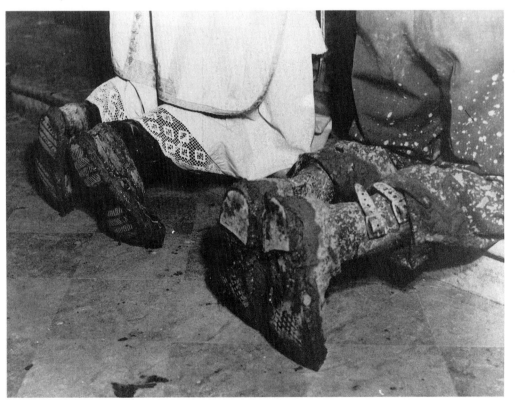

Left: Nicknamed 'Long Tom', the 155mm M1A1 gun on the M1 carriage could send a 95-pound shell up to 25,715 yards. The origin of this piece could be traced to WWI. This particular gun is being used near Nettuno, Italy, during February 1944, and has camouflage netting placed overhead to make it more difficult to spot by enemy aircraft.

Lower left: During a memorial Mass at San Benedetto, Italy, on 11 October 1944, a Catholic chaplain (on the left) wears a pair of spattered 12-inch shoe pacs, M1944 under his clean white linen alb, while the man who acts as his server has on snow speckled M1943 two-buckle boots.

Below: Life imitating art as a G.I. rolls up the sleeves of his 1943-pattern field shirt and strikes the pose of a French WWI *poilu*. His M1 carbine has the 15-round clip. This .30 calibre light weight semi-automatic gas-operated weapon served many purposes including for armoured personnel, officers, and parachutists. It had an effective range of 300 yards.

Left: In 1943-pattern field uniform these troops rest against a 1½-ton 6x6 cargo-personnel truck. Two of the men have goggles pushed up over their helmets while the man seated on the left has sunglasses. His M1 carbine has a canvas muzzle cover to keep dirt out of the barrel. A piece of webbing closed by a metal snap held this canvas 'US' stamped accessory in place, which gave way to simple cellulose tape toward the end of the war.

Right: Enduring the 'Battle of the Bulge', 101st Airborne intermingled with men of the armoured force dig out some of their comrades who have been trapped in the rubble of a bombed building. By this point (December 1944) most of the special airborne uniforms have been replaced by the more universal combat attire, including the 1943-pattern field jacket and trousers.

Left: Five members of the 534th Anti-Aircraft Battalion receive reading material in the St. Die area of France, during November 1944. The web rear strap and brown leather front strap for the M1 helmet particularly are visible on the man at the right, although these fastening devices seldom were worn attached under the chin to keep the helmet in place.

Below: Trudging along, during late December 1944, troopers of the 101st Airborne Division move out of Bastogne in a counter-attack after being under siege for ten days. Many wear the double-breasted wool overcoat and wool gloves liners against the winter temperatures.

Left: The shocking effectiveness of German winter camouflage uniforms first encountered in December 1944 originally prompted Americans to turn to local resources, such as adapting white materials with fine Belgian linen predominating until the quartermaster could begin issue of official gear. Here, 1st Infantry Division troops receive their issue of snow capes and hoods at Nidrum, Belgium, on 5 January 1945.

Left: Three 18th Infantry Regiment soldiers adjust their white snow capes in Nidrum, Belgium, during January 1945. These relatively inexpensive light-weight poncho style garments were just the thing to cut the wind and help a G.I. blend in with his surroundings. Unlike the trousers and parka, they were easier to manufacture and one size essentially fit everyone.

Right: The winter of 1944/5 also brought out white trousers of light weight cotton which were to be worn over the standard wool or 1943-pattern combat trousers and the reversible parka with white on one side and OD on the other to provide camouflage and to add extra protection against the cold. Conceived as garments for ski troops, these items were issued to regular infantry and airborne troops in the wake of experience gained at the Battle of the Bulge.

Below: By January 1945 some troops could enjoy a respite from fighting as in this instance of a corporal and a technical sergeant who offer a highly prized Coca Cola and Lucky Strike cigarettes to their new creation, 'Agnes', a snow woman whose attire is only slightly less formal than that of the two soldiers in their 1943-pattern field jackets. The sergeant (right) has on canvas ski-gaiters which were designed to be worn with mountain-ski-boots, although in this case standard service field shoes are being used.

Above: Inside the Siegfried Line three 'dogfaces' plant soil from their home state of California. The man on the left has stuck an M3 trench knife with what appears to be a slightly cut down M6 scabbard in his ammunition belt, while all three have on the pre-1941 style mackinaw with shawl collar. The outer garment was made of waterproofed tent shelter canvas with a 30-ounce wool lining.

Opposite page, top: Still fearing the enemy would use chemical warfare late in the conflict, VI Corps soldiers don gas masks of the type adopted and issued by 1944 and check their protective gear in a portable gas chamber somewhere in Germany, during February 1945. The staff sergeant at the far left has tucked what appears to be an

aluminium pommeled civilian hunting knife behind the russet leather holster holding his .45 caliber M1911A1 pistol.

Opposite page, bottom: Tending an unlikely patient, lst Glider Infantry, 17th Airborne Division, aidmen set the leg of a calf which was broken when it fell into a foxhole near Bastogne, Belgium, during January 1945. Two of the men have placed standard medic's brassards under the netting of their M1 helmets. The man on the left has on either the long sleeve 'V' neckline OD wool sweater or highneck worsted wool sweater with button neck closure issued starting in 1943, under his olive drab wool shirt, and has stabbed a bayonet for the M1 carbine in the ground leaving his M8 scabbard empty.

Left: Technician 4th Grade Jack Freeman, a member of the 34th 'Red Bull' Division's 175th Field Artillery, receives the Bronze Star from the division commander, Major General Charles Bolte. Freeman's initials appear on the side of his M1 helmet, just one of many markings G.I.s added to this protective piece of headgear. Freeman's khaki web waist belt holds up his olive drab wool trousers. The general's web M1912/17 magazine pocket for two .45 calibre clips for his automatic pistol are evident as is his M1924 first aid pouch.

Left: Keeping uniforms clean, even in a combat zone, was a challenge to maintain health and morale. At a Sicilian base of the 12th Air Force, Yankee ingenuity is pressed into service for this purpose, with a power driven washing machine made up of a tub taken from half of a French 55 gallon oil drum topped by a lid made from a German anti-aircraft searchlight, all operated by wooden paddles affixed to a German 88mm shell casing that ran from a one-half horsepower electric motor. Allegedly the contraption could handle a week's laundry for fifty men a day.

Right: Taken in January 1945, the private on the left wears an armoured soldier's winter cloth hood and carries a British Mk. II Sten sub-machine-gun. He is joined by his comrades from the 777th Field Artillery Battalion, an all African American unit during the period when the U.S. Army was still segregated. The aidman, distinguished by red Geneva Crosses painted on his helmet, holds a pair of heavy work gloves, atypical but practical accessories.

Right: Aidmen apply Carlisle field dressings and administer morphine to combat the results of a mine which has badly wounded one of the engineers serving with the 10th Armoured Division in Trier, Germany, in March 1945. The medic kneeling second from the left has stencilled his serial number on the top of his M1 helmet, while the medic on the far right wears the two-buckle M1943 combat boots with the 5-inch leather cuffs. Standing in the background centre an armoured soldier has on tanker's overalls and jacket but wears a standard M1 helmet with goggles rather than the composite, cloth, and leather tanker's helmet.

Left: Civilians officially accompanying troops also donned uniforms, such as this *Stars and Stripes* correspondent who has obtained a tanker's jacket which bears a black and yellow patch identifying him as a news reporter. Here he is speaking to Brigadier General Arthur Ruggles outside Rome, in March 1945. An officer stands behind him in an officer's model trench coat.

Above: Major General Roderick Allen, commander of the 12th Armoured Division, discusses test firing of tanks with Lieutenant-Colonel Paul Woods, an ordnance officer whose branch is indicated by the stenciled flaming bomb device on his helmet. Woods also has on a pile field jacket with its artificial fur interior. This garment was originally conceived of as a layer to be worn under the 1943-pattern field jacket but instead was used under overcoats and parkas as well as on occasion as an outer wear item as seen here. The general has elected to obtain a B-15 Army Air Force intermediate flight jacket.

Left: Captured German prisoners pass men of the 88th Division in Italy during April 1945. They are standing near an M4 Sherman tank, whose crewmen have donned M1 helmets in lieu of tanker style headgear, and who are wearing the standard 1943-pattern combat kit rather than special armour force garb.

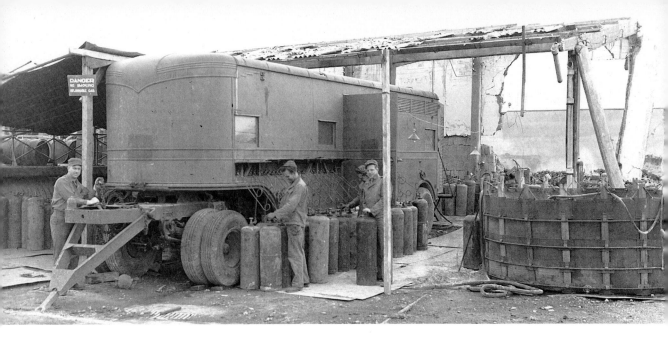

Above: Men from the 1049th Engineers set up a mobile acetylene plant in Naples, Italy, toward the end of 1944. They have on the pre-1943 HBT short-visor caps which were used to a great degree by mechanics and special troops in the ETO and favored by many soldiers operating in jungle environments in the Pacific and Asia.

Below: As they move up toward Prato, Italy, in April 1945, infantrymen of the 370th Regiment demonstrate the numerous ways ingenious G.I.s carried their equipment in the field. Packs, haversacks, and blanket rolls are all represented in the column.

Right: The hard-working 'halftrack' could haul troops and firepower over rugged, mired terrain as seen here in Germany's Hurtgen Forest where men of the 16th Infantry Regiment, lst Infantry Division, plow through, during February 1945.

Right: Moving at the rear of the column in France, during early 1945, a heavily modified M3A1 halftrack features an extended bumper, storage tanks on the rear and side, and a left-hand troop access door. Armament consists of the M2 .50 calibre Browning heavy air-cooled machine-gun and the M1919A45 .30 calibre Browning water-cooled machine-gun (to the right rear).

Right: The truck, ¼-ton, 4x4, was better known as the jeep. This multipurpose four-cylinder vehicle had a maximum speed of 65 mph. The jeep on the right has been modified with a stout wirecutting post mounted to the front bumper to snap wires stretched across roads by the Germans. A 'bustle' rack has been added to the jeep at the left which allowed extra equipment to be carried, thereby freeing interior space for personnel or more gear.

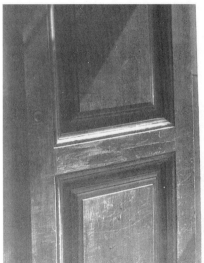

Left: During April 1945, Japanese Americans from the 442nd Regimental Combat Team (the most highly decorated U.S. unit of WWII) pile out of a jeep which has been rigged with what may be a DR4 wire reel to lay communication lines in Italy. In the background a second jeep bears the Red Cross marking which indicates that this particular vehicle was being used as a field ambulance, one of the many options for rugged four-wheel drive work horse.

Left: Flying a white flag with Red Cross, medics are ready to rush a wounded man from the 36th Infantry Division to an aide station in Haguenau, France, during March 1945. The shovel on the driver's side had many uses, including extracting the vehicle if it became bogged down in mud.

Left: Mounted on the M4 chassis and carrying a 155mm gun, the M40 represented one means to provide a division or corps with heavy artillery as seen here in Germany, during 1945. The self-propelled piece carried an 8-man crew at a maximum speed of 24mph. The gross weight was 82,000 pounds.

Right: To accommodate the growing number of women serving in the U.S. Army during the war an entire new wardrobe had to be developed including combat gear, as worn here in the case of First Lieutenant Elizabeth Bararcik, an army nurse who was stationed on the Western front for more than a year and a half. Her silver lieutenant bars are fastened to the shoulders of her field jacket and the Army Nurse Corps insignia is attached to the left collar of her olive drab shirt.

Right: In Liège, Belgium, Lieutenant Bernice Kondzielka of the 15th General Hospital looks prim and proper in her nurse's uniform as she checks a patient's blood pressure. More often than not this uniform gave way to more practical field garb when women served in combat areas.

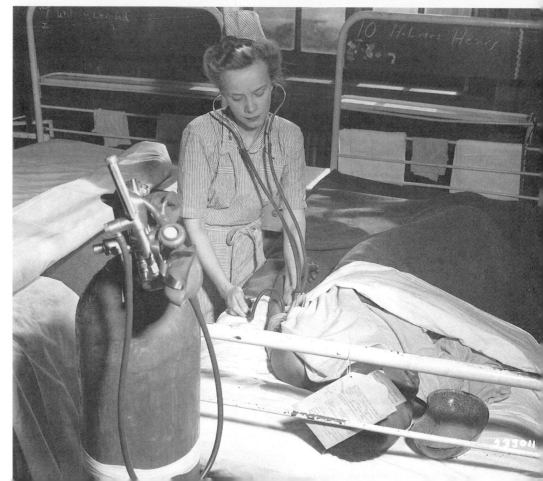

Left: Practicality not elegance was Lieutenant Edna Turfley's concern when she pulled on arctic 4-buckle boots and her 1943-pattern field jacket over her nurse's pinstriped uniform at the 10th Field Hospital in France, during February 1945.

Right: Members of the Women's Army Corps assigned to Twelfth Army at Verdun, France, appear in the version of the 1943-pattern field jacket designed for WACs and nurses. They all wear the M1936 dismounted leggings and field shoe, as well as OD wool field trousers. The private in the foreground has on a non-regulation sweater and kneels before a 'pup tent' formed from canvas shelter-halves, next to which is an up-turned M1 helmet without liner. In this configuration the headgear could be used as a wash basin or cooking utensil, thus contributing in part to references to it as a 'steel pot.'

Left: Another study in contrasts shows three U.S. Army nurses in Verdun, France, during October 1944, in their M1 helmets and 1943-pattern field jackets worn with their 'Class A' dark green skirt, brown shoes, and hose indicating that the area is relatively secure from front line fighting.

400131

Left: Private 1st Class Leo Des Champs of the lst Infantry Division calls in on his heavy back-mounted field radio at a crossroad in Kelz, Germany, during March 1945. Despite the late date both he and Technician 5 Edward Westley have on the pre 1943-pattern combat uniform.

Left: These 155mm 1945 'Easter eggs' bound for Hitler are going to be fired by U.S. artillerymen who wear the mixture of patterns which were available by the mid-1940s in Europe. The soldier on the left has on a 1943-pattern jacket and a pair of the 12-inch shoe pac, M1944, which were made of lined rubber bottoms with a leather top. The gunner at the right sports a Collins machete converted to a knife sheathed in a regulation M8 scabbard.

Above: Acting as an interpreter, Private 1st Class Nicholas Schaeffer interrogates a German POW, although his methods appear less than light handed. Schaeffer evidently has confiscated a few items from his charges because it appears that he has a pair of German cameras slung over his right shoulder resting on his left hip.

Below: Moving through Bonn, Germany, in April 1945, lst Infantry Division soldiers are ready for close fighting, particularly the man with the 'Tommy Gun' in the lead. This .45 calibre automatic submachine-gun could spray 600-725 rounds per minute. It came with twenty and thirty-round clips or could be used with a fifty-round drum magazine.

248431

Left: Private Gerald Cotton of the 1st Infantry Division, nicknamed 'The Big Red One' because of their shoulder sleeve insignia which dated to WWI, was part of the February 1945 assault across the River Ruhr. Loaded with spare bandoleers of ammunition, grenades, and the USN M26 life-preserving belt as well as U.S. Navy field glasses, he is ready for grim business. He carries the M1905E1 or an M1 bayonet in its M7 scabbard, both being standard for the M1 rifle.

Right: A light tank from the 1st Armored Division, the M5 or the M5A which was a redesign of the M3, heads toward Rome, in June 1944, just a few days before the Normandy landing. The tank's main gun was a 37mm M6 supported by calibre .30 machine-guns.

Right: River crossings also included Duplex Drive (DD) 'swimming' tanks which were M4A3 Shermans fitted with propellers to move them along once they drove into the water, as seen here on the left, during a March 1945 push into Germany. All sorts of collapsible boats and barges were used for this final phase of the war in Europe.

Left: With their lieutenant in front and a medic on the left, heavily laden combat troops make a river crossing towards enemy territory in the uniforms and equipment which had become standard as WWII came to a close in Europe, including Springfield rifles for sharpshooters.

Lower left: Poised on a raft, a G.I. raises his M1 Garand and takes aim at a suspicious object floating down river. He has on the 1943-pattern field jacket with the hood buttoned on.

Opposite page, top: River crossing, such as this one into Germany, could be assisted by the amphibious DUKW, a 30-foot-long seven-ton vehicle which could haul thirty-five men on land and fifty afloat, in which case a rear-mounted propeller drove the waterborne vehicle.

Below: A closer view of the DUKW demonstrates an uncommon use for this amphibious piece of equipment. Its hood serves as a pulpit while the chaplain of the 10th Mountain Division in Torboli, Italy, offers prayers of thanksgiving, on 3 May 1945, after the announcement of the unconditional surrender of all Nazi forces in the country. The crossed red bayonets on their 10th Mountain Division patches are visible on the left shoulders of many of the men, who otherwise wear the same uniform and gear as their counterparts in infantry units.

Above: The Browning air-cooled .50 calibre M2 heavy machine-gun was used both on vehicle and ground mounts. This 82-pound weapon could fire at the rate of 450 rounds per minute and could provide anti-aircraft protection, as seen here for a Bailey-bridge river crossing operation into Germany late in the war.

Right: Replacements for the 104th 'Timberwolf' Infantry Division in Germany, during March 1945, receive instructions about the operation of the BAR, a .30 calibre gas-operated weapon with a 20-round magazine that had a 500-600 round per minute rate of fire.

Opposite page, top: Representatives of the Dutch government decorate Major General Gavin, commander of the 82nd Airborne Division, with the Order of William, the highest combat award of that nation. Gavin's garrison or overseas cap is trimmed in gold for a general officer and bears the combined parachutist and glider patch as well as his two stars to indicate rank. His parachutist qualification badge (jump wings) is centred presumably on the oval red, white, and blue background color of the division headquarters.

Left: Brigadier General Arthur Rogers addresses infantrymen at Cechignola, Italy, as they attend a USO show shortly after the war has ended. He wears the officer's walking-out uniform which was known popularly as 'pinks and greens' because of the contrasting salmon coloured trousers (often of elastique) and dark green coat with matching cloth belt. Note the combat infantryman's badge above his ribbons.

Below: Other examples of the 'Class A' uniform in Italy, during April 1945, depicts the variations available, including an MP with white helmet liner, white leggings, and a Sam Browne belt.

U. S. ARMY CAP INSIGNIA

OFFICERS　　**OFFICERS—WAC**　　**WARRANT OFFICERS**　　**ENLISTED MEN**　　**ENLISTED WAC**

U. S. ARMY DIVERS

**U. S. MILITARY ACAD.
(West Point)**　　**OFFICER—Army
Transport Service**　　**OFFICER—Army
Harbor Boat Service**　　**DIVER, MASTER**　　**DIVER, 1st Cl.**　　**DIVER, 2nd Cl.**　　**DIVER, SALVAG**

U. S. ARMY INSIGNIA OF RANK—OFFICERS, WARRANT OFFICERS AND NON-COMMISSIONED OFFICERS

**GENERAL
OF THE ARMY**

MAJOR

**FIRST
SERGEANT**　　**MASTER
SERGEANT**　　**TECHNICAL
SERGEANT**　　**STAFF
SERGEANT**　　**TECHNICIAN
3rd GRADE**

CAPTAIN

**1st
LIEUTENANT**

GENERAL

**LIEUTENANT
GENERAL**

SERGEANT　　**TECHNICIAN
4th GRADE**　　**CORPORAL**　　**TECHNICIAN
5th GRADE**　　**PRIVATE
1st CLASS**

**MAJOR
GENERAL**

**BRIGADIER
GENERAL**

U. S. ARMY MINE PLANTER SERVICE
CUFF BRAID

**2nd
LIEUTENANT**

**CHIEF
WARRANT
OFFICER**

COLONEL

**LIEUTENANT
COLONEL**

Engineer

**Master Mine
Planter or Chief
Engineer**

**1st Mate Mine
Planter or
Ass't Engineer**

**2nd Mate Mine
Planter or 2nd
Ass't Engineer**

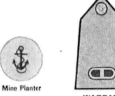
Mine Planter

**WARRANT
OFFICER**

**FLIGHT
OFFICER**

Above: WWII Cap and rank insignia for officers and other ranks.

THE ARMS—U. S. ARMY

THE SERVICES—U. S. ARMY

Above: WWII Officer's collar insignia.